I0336181

Copyright © 2021 by Adrian Laurent

All rights reserved. No part of this book may be reproduced or used in any manner without written permission of the copyright owner except for the use of quotations in a book review.

Limit of Liability/Disclaimer of Warranty:
This is a work of fiction. Names, characters, places, and incidents either are the product of the author's imagination or are used fictitiously. Any resemblance to actual persons, living or dead, events, or locales is entirely coincidental.

Although the publisher and the author have made every effort to ensure that the information in this book was correct at press time and while this publication is designed to provide accurate information in regard to the subject matter covered, the publisher and the author assume no responsibility for errors, inaccuracies, omissions, or any other inconsistencies herein and hereby disclaim any liability to any party for any loss, damage, or disruption caused by errors or omissions, whether such errors or omissions result from negligence, accident, or any other cause.

The information in this book is not intended to be used, nor should be used, to diagnose or treat any mental health or medical condition. For diagnosis or treatment of any mental health or medical condition, consult a licensed professional, psychologist or physician. Both the author and publisher of this book are not liable or responsible for any damages or negative consequences from any preparation, treatment, action, application to any person.

ISBN 978-0-473-60408-0 (EPUB)
ISBN 978-0-473-60406-6 (Paperback)

Bradem Press
New Zealand

www.adrianlaurent.com

Tim's Toddler Tantrum Story

Adrian Laurent

Tim loved playing with T-Rex. He raced T-Rex in his monster truck over a huge jump into a cushion-volcano full of lava.
"Mom! Dad! T-Rex jumped into the lava!" said Tim.
"That's nice, dear!" Said Mom.
"Can you watch!" Said Tim.
"Sorry, not now Tim. We're busy," said Mom.

Tim's face got red and his ears felt hot. His heart beat hard and his muscles got tight. Tim knew what was happening. He felt angry, but that was OK. He knew how to help the anger feeling go away.

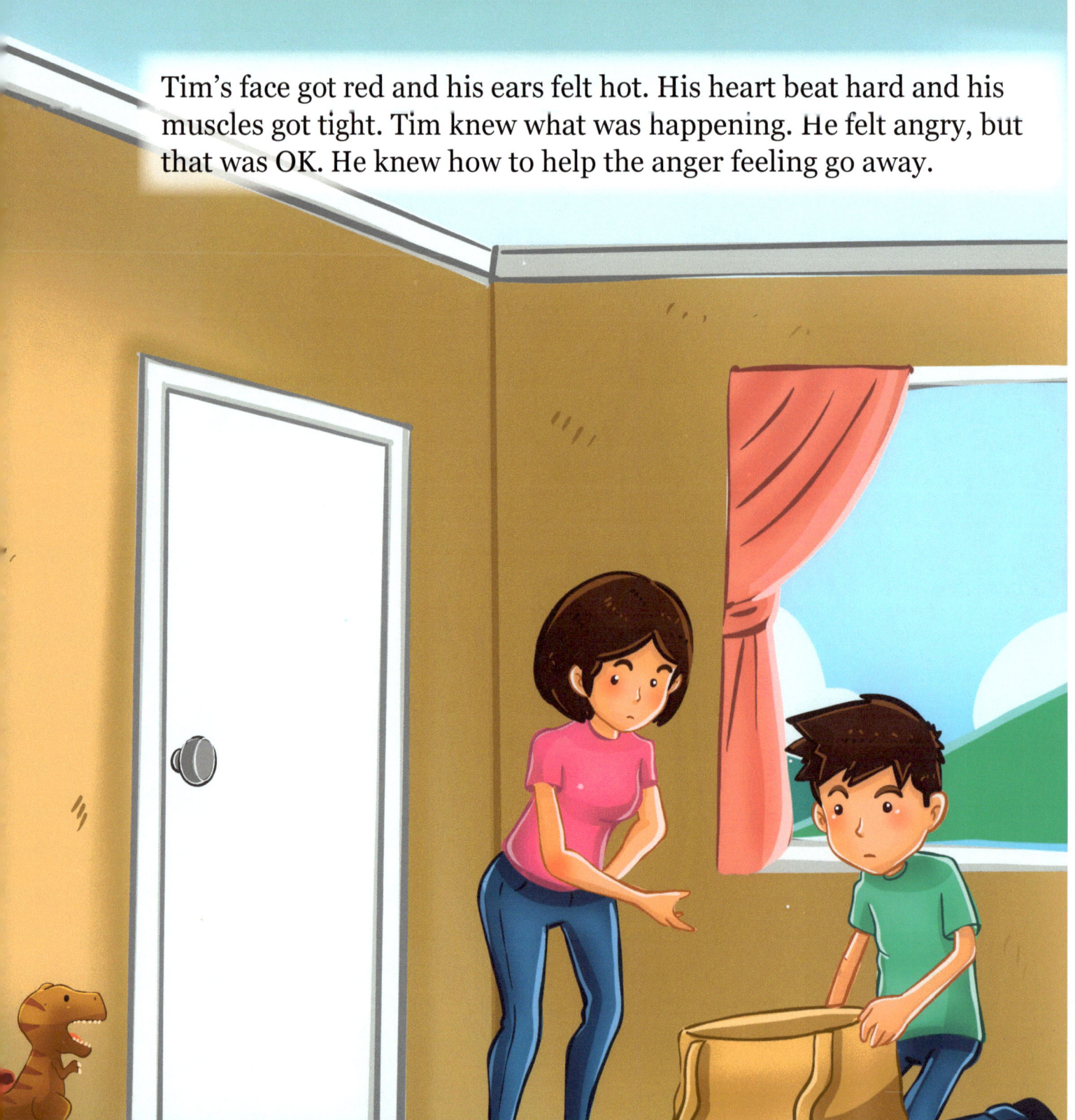

Tim counted to 10 and took big breaths in and out.
As he breathed and counted, he felt calmer.

Tim rescued T-Rex from the lava, then boosted it in the monster truck into the air.
"It's time to go Tim," Said Dad
"But I'm playing." Said Tim, frustrated.
"I'm sorry, Tim, we're going shopping." Said Dad.
"But I want to stay here and play." Said Tim.

Tim's face got red and his ears felt hot. His heart beat hard and his muscles got tight. Tim knew he felt angry, but it was OK. He knew how to make the anger go away. He squeezed T-Rex so tight it's eyes bulged. Soon he felt calm again.

They drove to the grocery store. Tim saw a chocolate egg with a surprise inside.

"Can I have one of these, Mom?" Asked Tim.

"No, Tim. Not now, sorry," said Mom.

Tim's face got red and his ears felt hot. His heart beat hard and his muscles got tight. Tim knew he felt angry, but that was OK. He knew how to make the anger go away.

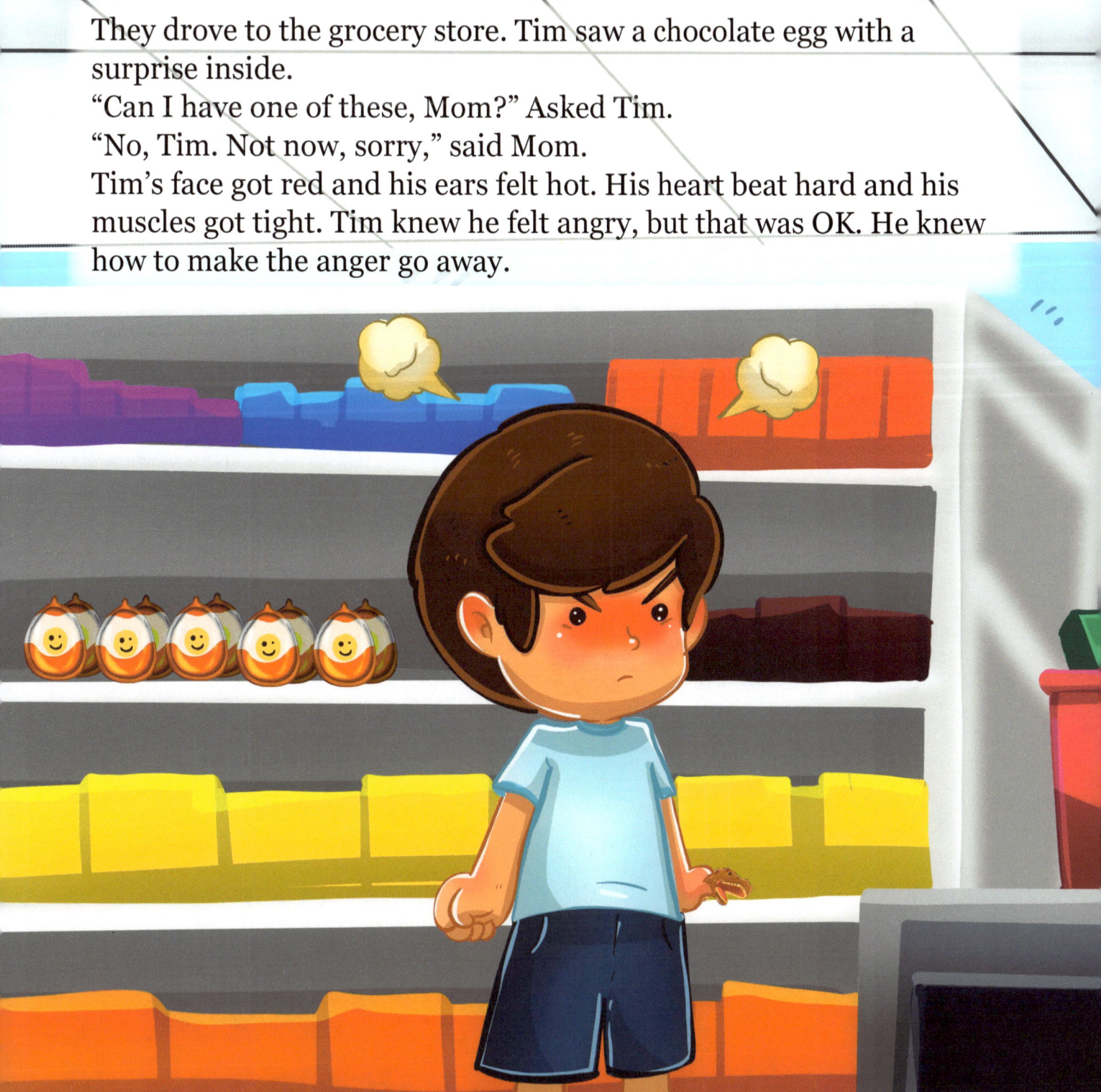

Tim traced his finger slowly around T-Rex while he breathed in and out. But Tim still felt mad.

"Tim, you're frowning," Said Dad. "It looks like you're having a hard time. Try using your words to tell us how you feel?"
"I feel mad and sad at the same time." Said Tim, crying.
"I feel like all day you have said no and I have felt angry. I felt ignored and couldn't play. I couldn't have chocolate. I feel frustrated!" Said Tim.

"I hear you, Tim." said Dad. "Today was busy, and I'm sorry we ignored you. Thank you for telling us how you feel. I understand you feel ignored and frustrated. How about we go to the park to play and eat some of these yummy apples?"
Tim's face lit up. "Yes!" he said.

They went to the park and played on the swings until the sun went down.
As they drove home, Tim said, "It's funny. I tried hard not to be angry all day. What helped most was telling you how I felt."

The End

I hope you enjoyed the story.

Feedback from fantastic readers like you help other parents find this book and give them confidence to choose it.

I would be so grateful if you could take one minute to leave your honest feedback about the book.

Thank you!

Adrian Laurent
Children's Book Author